DO THE MONKEY

Norma Cole

ZASTERLE
LA LAGUNA-CANARY ISLANDS
2006

Grateful acknowledgement to the editors of *Primary Writing* and *The Gig*, and to Elliot Anderson's CAMS project, where some of these texts first appeared.

ISBN: 84-87467-44-X

© 2006 by Norma Cole

Cover Art © 2006 by Pablo Siquier. *0606*. Carbonilla sobre papel. 120 x 146 cm. 2006.

First Edition

All rights reserved

Zasterle books are available thru
Small Press Distribution
1341 Seventh St
Berkeley, CA 94710-1403
(510) 524-1688

Zasterle
Apdo 167
38200 La Laguna
Tenerife – Canary Islands
Spain

Zasterle Books website: http://webpages.ull.es/users/mbrito/zasterle.htm

Printed and bound in the Canary Islands at El Productor S.L.

To Rob, Michelle & Jesse

*Before the mind catches up
the body's been and gone.*

no my hedge

it's not that I've reversed my vest

like all habits

I insist on it

to my knowledge

a butcher's work

keystone or plumstone

something I've learned to see

for Emmanuel Hocquard

The Olympics Is All in Your Mind

for Elliot Anderson

bluish-white, scarce ore, shaking and red splotches as if her leg was all bloody and then blood would drip on the rug and on the chair
calming, like a color, like blue, or calming like the pink of a child's room or a hospital corridor, pink pearl or a kind of peach color intending to be calming like the absence of discourse
you simply keep going as the shadows get long, twos and then threes and sixes until finally two enter(s) and one last one
but then some tentative foot placements, as if the floor was suddenly hot or covered with a fine layer of ground glass, fine as a powder
imagine the dancers to be in the room, in the room with the blue chair and blue air, sheet music strewn about

* * *

They left a long time ago.
Strides into the room.
Strides in this restricted space?
Stepped then, gingerly more likely. Entered gently, tentatively, stepping between the coffee table strewn with papers, possibly pages of street music, I mean sheet music, drafts or sketches of an unfinished piece, as yet untitled, sporadically thought and partially remembered.
Steps between the upholstered blue chair and the coffee table strewn with papers, then past the blue chair filled with blue air, appearing to aim for the sofa on the opposite side of the room, outside the frame. Debates about suing a rhetorical device, perhaps repetition or receptor theory, with variations, here, but lets the idea slip away out of the frame, over the falls in a barrel.
People were still pulling that prank over fifty years ago, before the beginning of her reign. The idea of her reign over a barrel over the falls.

* * *

The one not in the room at that time had been trying to organize an event, a spectacle patterned after his idea of the olympics as they once were. Nothing like the corporate sports events of today but rather more like an imagination of the *arche*, sports, arts, *arete*, competition and excellence, risk. This time they would be in a town he'd visited in Mexico. Or in Paris, in and around an abandoned automobile factory. With corporate sponsorship, or at least seed money. Tennis and Theater. What he enjoyed. What he enjoyed watching on the television, also outside the frame, in that room, from the couch or the upholstered blue chair, during the afternoon with the curtains drawn against the light like the light now, leaching out the color, the substance, the very forms from the room. Drafts of the proposal were piled uncollated on the coffee table near the blue inflatable chair. How to approach potential subscribers, he wondered.

* * *

Did she know that painting whose title was the same as her book? There is no evidence of painting or even books about painting in that room, only mirrors and, at times, smoke. They hadn't been all the way through the argument about meaning.

There might be examples, if individuals could be said to be examples, not of their gibberish, for that gibberish is something else, something they own and use to fill the room's vacancy with vacancy. But their lives are maps, they're rather the evidence of the rupture, both collusion and opportunism, homeostatic like the blue air, like the atmosphere in the room, the way it refers—it's a stretch—to the dream of B's double room, preposterously, providing documentation , occasional, posthumous but enduring, that is the hook.

When need or pleasure being mutually addressed, erase the surface indicators of favor, the power index

* * *

Nothing yet said about the place mat or the dark part of the chair back facing the desk, facing the wrinkled picture plane.

A young man placed his hands on my head, along the sides of my head and said come back in six days. I said I couldn't, or thought I couldn't. He thought, come back when you can. He gave me a turquoise umbrella when I left the room. It matched the chair. It might have been behind the chair.

The black suitcase is stored behind that chair. It looks identical to the one with writing all over it, Tibetan writing in white, like shoe polish, the liquid white shoe polish that comes in a plastic bottle with a sponge at the opening, under the cap, so you can brush the polish onto your white canvas shoes or white leather shoes once you've lifted them from under the other chair.

* * *

HEAVY LIFTING

> She doesn't want
> the bunchy look
> of male lifters
> *Diane Ackerman*

1.

She doesn't want
The small arena almost filled
When the fighters slow down, moving towards each other
My head so big

I need to train
I said to Joe Frazier
Here I am
I remember Sundays when the man I call my father made me

We play basketball
We play basketball
The dark scissors of his legs
Sometimes I feel like I will *never* stop

Please refrain from ogling your neighbor's penis
Stretch your hamstrings, think of how you are lifting
I'll be the first
If muscles are the currency of dreams

I go out to find whatever comes
I never told you
I caught a tremendous fish
Like a big peony

2.

It was too soon
I wanted to look
Against the colored horizon
I was happy enough

I forgot
Sand shifted in the undercurrent
Into the purples and oranges of reflection
As the sky went black, slowly

You never thought it would come to this
A man staring at a small lake sees
Didn't think of the clasp
God help me, liberal mothers

What's it like? You take it from me
Happy to have these fish!

3.

Caesar's Palace
Half asleep
It comes over and over
In 1948, the year I was born

I sat up straight in bed
I never played for you.
I have not slept for a week
Because he played games seriously

One woman has nothing out of place

4.

Sprawled belly-down on the damp planks
The approach to the bar is everything
I am the poet of the pinch shot the same as the fly-kill
I know I am robust

Half-numb, guzzling bourbon and Coke from coffee mugs
But why make a long story long?

5.

The heavy bodies lunge, the broken language watching baseball when the San Francisco Giants take the field we were drinking for free, bumming beers his art is eccentricity his aim in this soft age in my soft two bronzes into the change of autumn brush the elements have merged into solicitude half of America doubtless has the whole but supper's a small enough price to pay

Her face livened up but she was smart noses in the grave polloi that roiled baseball in the winter is our dream photos and clippings fade sugar dazzled too a sniff in the fallen air they come back now those nights my friend and I I like the articulate crack the little gussied-up bodies and terrible for anyone in his groove

6.

When we both walked out empty-handed
Mantle ran so hard, they said
The stadium is filled
I prayed for him to quit, before
We light the candles we were told to bring
He could help us out
Going up for the jump shot
A hook shot kisses the rim and
When the world finally ends
You can always spot them even from high up

7.

Am I really a sports fan I ask myself?
Is nothing real but when I was fifteen
A huge summer afternoon with no sign of rain.... Elm trees
Though the day is just breaking
We step out on the green rectangle
Never afraid of those huge creatures
It's thirty years ago

8. You go up there cocked

Each of them must have been terrified
Their center blocks out and the ball
Was balanced on the edge of the platform
Fanaticism? No. Writing is exciting
Thank God

9. As the man next door on his porch

At eight I was brilliant with my body
After practice: right foot
Most mornings I get away, slip out
That one long year we moved
There are so few photographs of him
Like the other day in Detroit
The pitcher shot her husband
The high hard one – up
Bravado among cars, tempting fate
The river turns
For years I've watched the corner for signs
These days
I stop

10.

The gun full swing the swimmer catapults and
The beautiful excess of Jesus on the waters
In the end when the doctors circle around
The sun rising over the mountains
I'm back after twenty years of baiting the trap of the past
You are tired

When you get there
Be perpendicular to the basket

"HEAVY LIFTING: POEMS LIFTED LINE BY LINE"
(from *motion: American SportsPoems*,
Edited by Noah Blaustein. University of Iowa Press 2001)

The Catastrophe

This is strange tongue in the form of a heart where atoms of color dance, colors of manifestations on the soft ground of conscience. This is an illustrated fish, a little blue fork or prongs as incarnations. This is a bucket of energy, a barred spiral. This sand bar permits the passage of blood with variations, horizontal. Light. This light is on a dark blue ground or a deep red ground or a midnight green ground, a disk of dancing metal arrows, all show. Ruling colors of the spiral, precipitous, terrifying, an ancient treaty. Give up the idea of the state. Can it be said? To whom can it be said? To someone's father or mother? The world, night, demolition of homes, control of water. Lack of water. Build and destroy. Trial. Walls of the moat or the room, their design and multiplication, constant dialogue of light and shade. Narrow verticals. Rise. All rise. Rare and free. Or rather free. A little free. An image of redefining, explicit, the point of the arrow, head down. Twice the energy. Little known and less represented. Observed in various visible forms, clarity, display. Evolving. The many. The tongue as haptic form evoking that principle.

NASDAQ NASCAR

for T R

        thick psycho circuit
        history re asphalt
        and the plains
        herm

        herm
        'n
        neutics
        rails and simple
details, seen   with x-ray vision

        using a mirror
        to hold down the corner
        or physical tabletop -- go
        boy, go
        report to nature

The head of a man rises out of the objects twice.
        The whole country is a bed with an ocean on either side.
Having put ties on them to extend them in the event.
        In the event the ink not dries.
Not flows, "inksetter" is the name.
        The mash.
Cyclone of again.
        On the assumption that drawing always returns.

ACTION

For in our actions we are not passively aimed like a gun, we are not passively straightened like a tablecloth.
Hendrik Walter

a cloud? a clown? a cloud of
singing frogs?

...learning to read in secret...
as a surprise, so reading
offered as a gift? a sculpture
come alive, talking and singing—
white face painted red red mouth

eyes?

"sorry to take away your bookmark"

    Making up
the mind
Q-How do you know when it's done?
Q-Is it done?
like sugar, like coke?

     conventions

The banality of code (any code) define
are required in order to define the un-
containable/boundless rhythms, the body
of the attempt, the outcast, other
collaborations?

Seeing history every day what does it mean? And the other is a shadow wing. And the person doesn't arrive because: doesn't return: doesn't find the place: arrives but doesn't identify the other: does identify the other but changes his mind: after all: the person behind the counter is smiling in spite of the violence: everything: the sleeping bag, finally the dress: arrives: that banishment of all prior speculation

Action ~~speaks and~~ still is.
This time, the flowers left on the roof of the car.
Day, reusable? The sky, astounded by
or astonished by the sky such as it is
or I could have done otherwise?
Days are always the first to know.
Take the show by the middle

       figure/ground   vs   field
         "subject"   subject?

paper under skin, skin, sound, outstanding in the pattern, lamplit on the Ruby Range

    TRACE, tracework, the farther that falls —"SOUND A WAY"

         pass a time

                         calamity, or the structure of thought

alerting her, they don't usually die of it.
They constructed the arena at the end of the first century and it was active until the third, the date of the first destruction of the city. The stones were then removed. They were then reused to construct the foundations and the walls of the next city where the population sought refuge. At that time the amphitheater became the burial ground.

in the other pattern for the sound, but it's not what I
mean. There, I've said it.

A Waka*

My dog Stoutie is a stout little pal, kind of sugary, damp little nose, especially when he wants to go for a waka.

*Japanese 31-syllable poem form

FLOATING BY

for David Bowie

"abundant" and "not true" somehow sets up the sound (elements active, activating, enacting, selecting)

somehow sets up the tides of sound that convincingly present "unchanging" as asking for "heaven" it's from my first body, actually, carrying them in
> but his is a strange and unheard of polish made of
> distance and intimacy

> GO BACK ONCE

>> the young falconer holding a hawk,
>> marvered glass eyes, threw his
>> shoulder into the heart of another
>> gilt heart

the solar systems that the song remembered, within the outside world, referred light, an image called thought to the place beyond "it's grave inside my head too"

> *amrita*, elixir of
> immortality almost
> recognize losing
> return, turning

DON'T KILL THE DUST

dotted rhythm of disruption
dust off "bewilderment"
silent window, free radio
of "our" youth "I meant it"
deepest thought – I did

these things are real, unguessed in air, child of science, of space, universe: is there a 5th dimension? can time run backwards? can love be lost?

hOULeS

New Orleans, 15 November 2002

orthorexia

I thorax ore

He haxe root

O hair to rex

+

aerobicist

I ciber toast

Rose tibiac

Sit arice o

=

Toast to Rex

he haxe root o hair
I thorax ore I ciber
rose tibiac o sit
arice

Units for Tomorrow

The fighting fish at first looks just like a fish.   The picture of evolution in the strangeness of what was occurring.   We didn't know.   In the vivid familiarity of our lives.   What was happening at the payphone.   It wasn't yet known.   It was a time of exuberant niches hit across.   An unexpected and burgeoning.   In a squat.
        Source of which.   Not yet a test for it.   Photons and compressed air.
        A continuous scansion of the inner ear.   The outer world symbolic sociophysical universe in order to discover. Where to adapt.   To reset what was out of kilter.   The unaccountabilities.   Our collision will be elastic.   Importation into it.
In general the pattern for the time.   Dearest Mae. Time to go.   We are battered.
        So this letter is wet.   A conversion myth.   Oops, readership.   "Inescapable morphology" what's yours?   Dropping slowing cutting across Rossetti's dream "I said the water was choppy."   Attack, decay.   The body slop.   The birthday came and went.   The picture the vividness.   Flowers on the hillside and the stench of burning flesh, the reporter said.   In the shantytown.
        You have a sweet voice, une voix douce, una dolce voce,

Saint Ives	Grasse	
Lands End	Vence	Bar du Loup

At a prayer site in the cemetery on a burial ground and relocation on paper.   On paper, for generations, for the future, on your bread, on your back, in your practice, at present no explanation undevourable at the barbecue, at a friend's, in the house before the movers come, at the table, on the carpet, at the beach, in a dream, reading, in the city

It was my faucet I was looking up. What I want is inviolate. "delirium of reason. It sets its sights on paradise (glorified generality)." a camel with a tiny saddle, a spare tire, turn viridian, grey fingernails arranged in a fan on the waiting-room wall: rain, ocean, heart, night, stream, glow between.   People sleeping in the house.

IN MEMORIAM JACQUES DERRIDA

> There is no Waste Land.
> Jessie L. Weston

Monkeys!?! Are they all
<u>monkeys</u>?
Tired monkeys.

D'you know that during the rococo
period
       —of the eighteenth century
you monkeys were given a new
identity by representing the
exoticism of the Far East
       —I would fain hope…

Verily, kiddo, I walk
among monkeys as among
the foreskins and limbs
of monkeys—monkeys
in ruins.

gala or apocalypse,
apocalypse or

a part of the body, a
secret part

But let's go for a moment to
the great ecumenical current
the discovery or the great
unveiling—I kid you not—
the ear whispering under its veil of hair—
or the milky way—study the tone
itself—

(I kid you not) the clock
chimes midnight—bong bong bong etc.
what changes a tone, what
causes a rupture of tone? How
does one distinguish—

He was just starting to get to the
Heideggerian conjugation of the
personal. La! Re-signing himself.

Come, come.

Then his
signature will have taken place.

His signature has
taken place.
Monkeys—love 'em or leave 'em.

Dear Robert,

    Hi, just wanted to check in
with you, see what's happening. I
was reading your "ACHILLES' SONG,"
the first poem in *GROUNDWORK:
Before the War* in which Thetis
promises Achilles not a boat
but the mirage of a boat. There is
always a "before the war," isn't
there. Some war. Another war.
Miss you.
           Love,

                Norma

P.S. and back of that war
"the deeper unsatisfied war"

THE BODY IS SOFT

> J'ai plus de souvenirs que si j'avais mille ans.
> *Baudelaire, "Spleen"*

full sea

outside the self

doesn't matter if it's real or not.
suddenly you aren't one of them
any more

apple, table or hand

the pink sky

"...the magnificence of it."
(Robert Duncan)

+

the arrival of sound

the rawness under the skin

while read

Funny Sunday, or A Word

"carry" at the grave
sight of redness

under the skin

the mute universal

concrete operations: their life
was social enough

come here

Who's Helen?

+

Rascal

seeking to be
matched with
reality

PAVEWAY

           (laser)

marked/formed

using flares as
decoys until they
gone

+

declensions

"simple travellers"

     (*L. Sterne*)
work done by hand,
by eye

outstript
that is
the work

the camera sees
all the way down

+

my face as well
as my house

so no matter how you
look at it

the opposite of
sweet homage

distance I
I watch distance

+

special powers

but the body is soft

"We write in sand"
   (*Edmund Waller*)
nak ta ancestors

everything is
in play

+

placing myself in the _____

tension & attention

"(the sacred furrow, the towers of
sand, and so forth)"
     (*David P. Chandler*)

named "dog" "imperfect" "red
in the face" "loves justice" "Dharma" or
flower names for girls
  = slave names

lightning will guide you

+

leapt off a leaf

is the next step

the emblem of the
endless problem

sticks with heads
  braided ribbons
but the marshes are gone

> "Weighed in the balance, hero's dust
> Is vile or vulgar clay"
> (*Lord Byron*)

swoons and staggers

"like before" or like
"before"
(just) anyone you've never met

+

wall, dear, floor

house of light like a loom
mutable will, house of hope

tree boxcar light
water   thunder

narrative is
the body
so breathe

the means to go back

on the other side of
what wax cylinder

oma mori (wish sack, Japan)
god is mental

+

mukei "formless"

ground to a halt? new
or hiatus

"Entrare nell'Opera"
                (*Giovanni Anselmo* 1971)

the mystery bank, a dearth
of self

He talked about the cool
fragrant fields in the early
morning, going out to pick
beans.

Monday, sound post
towards the end of body
art found wanting

+

drive time

but the body is sand
or glass—the mutational
corporation

on a low concrete structure
by the water, nursing the baby

freedom= rough "participation"

lay claim to hand and foot
the double feature, the third hand

his right hand
              the Nurse
         the native land

+

Epimetheus

of objects as of
bodies

braiding and nesting

they want to be kisses

accordingly
community that
finds itself
as image

suffered from time madness

these kinds of displays
a fiction or a treatise

such days have always
been a dream

+

string theory
tableaux

the free will again

no one
elected them

a dispute to which
one returns "I didn't
do that"

to all the people in
the country

a string of beads
or maybe pearls

\+

Observatory Time

what if my two hands
in your life

sensory drives motor

gestures? the army
    already (drew a
    blank) <u>fired</u>
    on the crowd
next thing you know

not showing all
sides of any
one thing

\+

that window "uchronia"
(memory under construction)

overlooking the immaculate
thingamajig

the pencil of nature
the tangled antennae

the polis hermetic
beloved machines

scuds rubber sirens
burning cloud

+

minutes pass

their leaves were moving
a do-it-yourself kit

has moved away
gray rust blue
pink blue

buku laut
a fish called Book
of the Sea

the shining in
the brain: do we
have a dream

on earth and time

+

other passwords

signal a
kind of second
sight or maybe
the air

and the partly cloudy
fullness thereof

the annunciation "I came here
for the signs"

lateral reading
working hand, eye

+

remember the night

the Café Aqueduct
the book is

a remainder
of the next book

view of the lake
red-tailed hawk
flying over

the light is your
night too

+

the shapes, feel
them
momently random

memory becomes
expectancy
"as witnessed by"

our wars
the findings

(fr)agile
slicing a lemon

a form of motion
a finishing

+

*Before the mind catches up
the body's been and gone.*

no my hedge
it's not that I've reversed my vest
like all habits
I insist on it
to my knowledge
a butcher's work
keystone or plum stone
something I've learned to see

Sarabande

"and then looks at
the stars" from the
bed in the ambulance

looks up at boughs of
trees shifting quickly
lit in blackness

blackening soft, deep
siren's song—she died
several times that night

and only in the weeks
to come started and
started to come back

then forward which is
real life

Do the Monkey by Norma Cole
is published by Zasterle in an
edition of 300 copies. 40 copies
belong as property to
Norma Cole.
10 copies have been signed by
the author. They may be
purchased from the publisher at
$20.00 per copy.